SCENIC NAMIBIA

SUNBIRD PUBLISHING

First published 2000
2 4 6 8 10 9 7 5 3 1
Sunbird Publishing (Pty) Ltd
34 Sunset Avenue, Llandudno, Cape Town, South Africa
Registration number: 4850177827

Publisher Dick Wilkins
Editor Brenda Brickman
Designer Mandy McKay
Production Manager Andrew de Kock

Reproduction by Unifoto (Pty) Ltd, Cape Town
Printed and bound by Tien Wah Press (Pte) Ltd, Singapore

TITLE PAGE The river bar at the Katima Mulilo's Zambezi Lodge.

LEFT The grand formations of the Fish River Canyon.

BELOW Namibia's desert elephants hurry to a water hole.

OPPOSITE The Ugab Valley Terraces east of Khoirixas.

Introducing Namibia

From a land where much of its wilderness is parched by the African sun rises a scenic beauty that is, although in places stark and unforgiving, quite breathtaking in its simplicity. From the golden dunes of the great Namib to the bone-white sands of its magnificent coast, the landscape here is one of enchantment, broken only by a desert mirage, a flock of grazing sheep, or a lone *Welwitschia mirabilis* on a distant horizon that forms a neat divide between the hot sand and a brilliant blue sky.

The many faces of Namibia – a nation that takes its name from the searing sands of the Namib that covers

BELOW A lone gemsbok (oryx) bull crosses the sea of sand that is the great Namib-Naukluft.

much of its landscape – represent a world of changing colours, a myriad different panoramas and a people who, despite an often troubled path toward independence and self-determination, have embraced this diverse land.

Of all its spectacles, the most extraordinary of Namibia's vistas is the long stretch of sand that comprises the great Skeleton Coast, an eerie expanse of beach that reaches from the country's northernmost border with Angola to the south, where it meets up with the dry and dusty plains of the Namib Desert in the Namib-Naukluft National Park. Flanked on the west by the cold waters of the Atlantic and on the east by the dry hinterland, this place of solitude covers 1.6 million hectares that, together, form the Skeleton Coast National Park, an extensive wilderness roughly divided into two main sections. While neither section is blessed with much mammal life – although any number of birds flit and soar across their skies – both remain extremely important, and in places, rather sensitive ecological areas that depend on a perfect balance within their fragile ecosystems. The northern reaches are covered by the sandy dunes of the Namib, but the gravel plains of the southern parts are liberally sprinkled with boulders and rocks and laced, on occasion, with rivers, the volatile nature of which bring little relief to this apparently barren coast.

Neatly bordered by the Kunene River in the north and the Hoanib in the south, the immediate interior from the northern strip of the Skeleton Coast is commonly known as the Kaokoland. The nearly 50 000 square kilometres of rough roads and endless stretches of

ABOVE The coast of the Namib-Naukluft Park, between the waters of the Atlantic and the sands of the Namib.

rocky, mountainous terrain – after which the Herero-speaking people named the area – are not immediately inviting to the traveller. The great Kunene is the home of fearsome crocodile, the tracks are difficult and unpredictable, and the landscape wild and, to a large degree, empty of inhabitants other than the local Himba people. Unfortunately, a ruthless drought in the 1970s ravaged the Kaokoland, reducing its wildlife population to pitiful levels and further destroying tireless conservation efforts that have been instituted to save the natural environment of the region. At the same time, however, the elephant population of this 'wasteland' continues to draw visitors and the Kaokoland remains a rather popular tourist destination.

To the northeast, on the other hand, stretches the 'big place of dry water': Namibia's Etosha National Park, a wide pan of some 5 000 square kilometres resting on the plains of this northern region and quite desolate in both appearance and mood. The conservation area centres around the salty pan of the same name that was once a nourishing lake and vital source of life for the animals and plants that inhabit the area. Today, although the pan is often no more than a semi-arid depression within the sand, it is virtually the only source of life for the wildlife that converges at its seasonal waters, allowing for a remarkable display of the capabilities of both the African veld and the living creatures that make their home here.

BELOW The Himba people and their customs and traditions remain a fascinating element of Namibian society.

Nestled between the great Etosha National Park and the Angolan border lies what was commonly referred to as Owamboland, which, together with Kavango and the narrow 'peninsula' that is Caprivi, forms Namibia's green northern belt. This vast area is blessed with a rainfall far more abundant than anywhere else in this sun-baked land. The landscape here is lush and green, carpeted with farmland and inhabited by a huge proportion of the country's total population, many of whom are the Owambo people, who give this region its name. Although a hotbed of militant struggle during the fight for Namibia's independence, this region is considerably more hospitable to the tourist, and yet it remains largely unappreciated by the traveller and thus surprisingly unaffected by the general upturn in tourism currently being enjoyed by the country as a whole.

The land covered by what was once known as Owamboland is, in most parts, planted with subsistence crops such as sorghum and millet, and is dominated by the relatively large town of Ruacana, home of the hydroelectric plant that feeds much the country. Kaoko is much the same: laced with tracks and roads largely unaccustomed to tourist traffic and peopled with locals who, although they spend much of their day farming the rich soils, are expert craftsmen, producing remarkable handiwork much in demand by the visitors who do explore this northern band of Namibia.

The Caprivi strip, steeped in colonial history and, in fact, named in honour of Imperial Chancellor, Count Leo Von Caprivi, is only some 50 kilometres at its widest point and is enveloped by four other nations: Botswana in the south, Zimbabwe in the east, and Zambia and Angola to the north. Much of these plains is covered by the Caprivi Game Park, some 600 000 hectares of conservation land most noted for its impressive

ABOVE Black-faced impala gather at Etosha's Klein Namutoni water hole.

population of elephants. But perhaps the most intriguing portion of land within the strip is the Golden Triangle, ancestral home to groups of indigenous San and others who crossed the Kunene and settled here following the turmoil of the Angolan civil war.

Once known as Bushmanland – when the San were settled here in the 1960s – the flat, dry Tsumkwe district comprises savanna, shrub- and woodland skirting the Kalahari, yet remains a home for the small San communities that, despite years of displacement and persecution, continue to live off the land in much the same way as they have done for centuries. The crowning glory of these plains is the occasional pans that dot the veld, attracting as they do the game species that congregate here to quench their thirst at the close of the annual dry season.

To the west of Tsumkwe lies the Waterberg Plateau and its parkland, and beyond stretches the old Damaraland, which, in turn, borders the Skeleton Coast.

Damaraland, the arid western plain sliced by the occasional river valley, is dominated by such remarkable landmarks as the 600-metre Spitzkoppe mountain range, the mining town of Uis, the rock-art treasures of Twyfelfontein, and, chief among them, the nearly 2 800-metre granite massif of the Brandberg. The area now falls within the boundaries of the modern-day Kunene and Erongo regions, but political boundaries do not influence the timeless wanderings of the gemsbok and springbok that traverse the plains, the klipspringer, dassies and jackal that clamber over its outcrops, and the birds that cross its skies.

Conveniently positioned between the hot sand of the Namib Desert in the south and the carcass-strewn shore of the Skeleton Coast extending northward is the city of Walvis Bay, unofficial capital of coastal Namibia. The lack of fresh water on this strip of coast meant that it held little interest for colonial powers for 300 years, but

BELOW The town of Walvis Bay is bound on the west by the Atlantic Ocean and on the east by the Namib Desert.

when conquering powers discovered the potential of its bay – Walvis boasts the deepest harbour in southwestern Africa – occupational forces vied for supremacy here, with the British, Dutch, Germans and South Africans all wielding control at some time during the country's often troubled past.

Walvis Bay, and the islands that lie off its shore, was finally reintegrated into the new nation of Namibia in 1994, and is a vital link in the country's economy, its port servicing both freight and the all-important fishing vessels. The city itself centres largely around the activities of the harbour and while there is not much for the tourist in the line of cultural and social activity – although it does claim to have a vibrant nightlife – there is plenty of opportunity for adventure. Tucked between the desert and the beach, Walvis Bay is an ideal centre from which to explore these starkly contrasted wildernesses, and the wetlands on the outskirts of the city boast a bird paradise of pelicans, flamingoes and any number of other avian species.

Both Lüderitz and Swakopmund, on the other hand, are entirely different. Charming in their features and, say some, graceful in character, these towns are a melting pot of the many influences – German and otherwise – that have traversed their paths over the centuries. Endowed with a moderate climate, a proud heritage and a gentle sophistication, Swakopmund and, to some degree, Lüderitz, are the country's only true holiday destinations. As such, both are extremely hospitable, catering for travellers of every description, from backpackers to self-drive adventurers to families and businesspeople – although Lüderitz, heart of the diving industry (both for diamonds, for which Namibia is world renowned, and seafood delicacies such as crayfish, or lobster), may demand a little more effort to reach than peaceful Swakopmund.

ABOVE The heights of the Spreetshoogte Pass offer an apparently endless vista of the edges of the great Namib.

The gentle charm of Swakopmund, however, does not detract from its competitor in the tourism stakes – the capital, Windhoek. Windhoek is everything that its coastal rival is not. Whereas Swakopmund invites the laidback traveller with visions of wide, open spaces and images of a natural wonderland of dune and sea, Windhoek is the Big City. Although hardly comparable to other world capitals, both in size and in stature, Windhoek is indeed a city, with a momentum of its own. It is busy, vibrant, and colourful – an economic heartland and financial powerhouse in its own right.

But, despite everything that these unique little towns and surprisingly intoxicating cities may offer, it is the vast natural heritage that remains Namibia's strongest – and most impressive – drawcard. And it is the rolling sands of the great Namib Desert that provide the overriding image of the Namibian landscape: row upon row of red-painted dune, interspersed only occasionally with some sparse vegetation and the flourish of a winding adder as it makes its way across the searing wilderness. This endless expanse covers some 16 per cent of Namibia's landscape, and embraces within its borders the Skeleton Coast and Namib-Naukluft parks, together comprising more than 6.5 million hectares of dry and arid land.

On the higher ground that forms the plateau further inland is one of Africa's most remarkable natural wonders, the extraordinary sculptural masterpieces that together form the great Fish River Canyon. The steep inclines and roughly hewn rockfaces of the canyon, eroded over time by the forces of nature and its ravaging elements, are second only to the Grand Canyon of North America. It is a wild and spectacularly unspoilt

BELOW The craggy formations of the Spitzkoppe near Usakos epitomise the nature of the Namibian landscape.

wilderness of geological formations carved from layers of sandstone, shale and lava over a period of some 1 800 million years. The canyon itself is just over 160 kilometres long and, in parts, nearly 600 metres deep, but its grandeur lies more in the spectacle than in the unfathomable geological records and data that make up this natural phenomenon.

However, whereas the Fish River Canyon comprises layer after layer of rock sliced through by valleys and gullies, the vast Kalahari that lies to the east and beyond is mile after mile of endless sand laced with dry riverbeds and punctuated by the occasional camel thorn tree. These scanty grasses and undulating dunes of the desert-like Kalahari, reaching south into South Africa and east into Botswana, are home to a surprising array of wildlife, that thrives under this harsh sun and rejoices at the spring rains that bring respite to the dry veld, transforming for just a short while the relentlessly harsh wilderness into a green wonderland. This great thirstland takes its name from the Setswana word *Kgalagadi*, which varies in translation from 'the dry land' to 'the land that has dried up' – in any event, a most appropriate name for such a vast and far-reaching expanse of apparent desolation.

The great frontier that cuts between Namibia and its southern neighbour, South Africa, is the mighty Orange River, a natural boundary that extends for some 500 kilometres between the two countries.

En route from the interior – where it originates in the mountainous highlands of Lesotho – the Orange snakes through some of the wildest terrain on the subcontinent, slicing through rock-strewn veld and barren sands as it makes its way to the vast Atlantic Ocean in the west. The river itself – which takes its name from the Dutch prince William of Orange – extends for some 2 000 kilometres in total, and in parts some seven kilometres in width, traversing

ABOVE A small herd of wild horses have made their home on the sands of the Namib.

ever-drier lands until it reaches the raging ocean at Oranjemund – the Dutch for 'mouth of the Orange' – which, in turn, is the centre of Namibia's lucrative diamond-mining industry. As southern Africa's most impressive water course, the Orange is not only a spine along which stretches thousands of kilometres of delicate ecological regions, each with its own unique qualities and demands, but is also a centre for adventure sports that attracts huge numbers of thrill-seekers intent on battling the sometimes torrential waters on canoe or raft.

From the rampant waters of the Orange River, the parched lands of the Namib and the unforgiving wilderness of the Kalahari to the humble traditions of the Himba, the colourful dress of the Herero and the gentle giants that are the desert elephants, these are the images of Namibia. It is the rolling dunes, the shifting sands, the gushing rivers, the dry riverbeds and the age-old skylines that have made a remarkable island of tranquillity in the sometimes harsh sea that is Africa.

Scattered along the extensive coast of Namibia are colonies of Cape fur seals that visit the sands of the Skeleton Coast from the often icy waters of the Atlantic. The seals, numbering in excess of 600 000 individuals, beach in huge numbers to calve and nurse their pups here and to bask on the rocky shores. These mammals give birth to one, and occasionally two pups at a time. Enormous concentrations comprising huge colonies may be found up and down the coast, with the most numerous at the Cape Cross Seal Reserve – some 120 kilometres from Swakopmund – and off Bird Island, south of Walvis Bay.

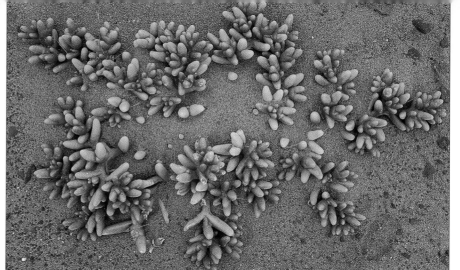

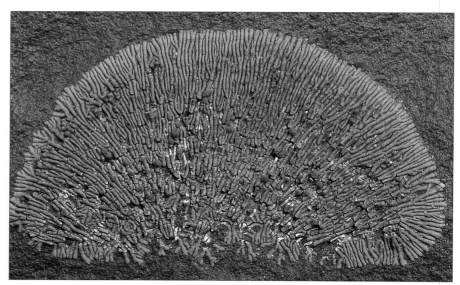

LEFT Namibia's apparently barren Skeleton Coast nevertheless boasts a unique array of life.

TOP Most desert plants, such as this mesemb, are succulents, which depend on moisture gleaned from coastal fog, rather than on the cycle of the rains.

ABOVE Localised species of lichen, such as *Caloplaca namibensis*, drape themselves over hardy rock surfaces to form a patchwork of colour and shapes.

OPPOSITE Like the parched crust of earth that, in times of rain, carries the water of the Huab River, much of the Namibian landscape is dry and inhospitable.

LEFT Despite the aridity of the broader region, the Namibian coast and, indeed, certain inland areas, are home to diverse water birds that nest and forage in and around vital water sources. This avocet, with its contrasting plumage – dark above and light beneath – is on the hunt for prey in the still waters of the Skeleton Coast.

ABOVE Often seen in flocks of hundreds that huddle in congregations on the water's edge, white pelicans are a common sight on the coastal reaches of Namibia, where they skim the waters for fish prey and dot the skies overhead as they take flight.

OPPOSITE An immature black-winged stilt, with its distinctively long legs and sharp, pointed beak, wades through the water, foraging for food. These waders occur in the marshes, floodlands and even saltpans throughout much of southern Africa.

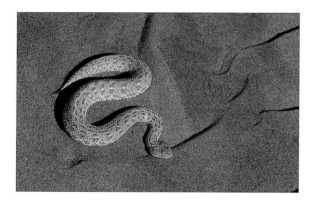

TOP LEFT Like many of the reptiles of the Namib, the horned adder is a terrestrial species that has adapted well to the harsh conditions of the desert.

CENTRE LEFT Peringuey's adder, in its sideways-gliding movement across the desert sands making typical tracks easily identifiable as those of this snake, is, understandably, often more commonly known as a sidewinding adder.

LEFT The shovel-snouted lizard, with its distinctly flat-ended mouth, is endemic to the Namib Desert and has a unique bladder-like receptacle in which it stores water taken from the fog-laden sand.

ABOVE Although the Namaqua chameleon is not unique to Namibia, this terrestrial species has also developed unique methods to cope with life on these searing sands. It will change its coloration to black to absorb the heat in the cold mornings, and then become paler to reflect the sun of the afternoon.

OPPOSITE The shifting dunes of the Namib and its surrounds, ever on the move and always changing face, are the home territory of an extraordinary array of wildlife: from snakes and other reptiles to small mammals, birds and insects, and all contribute to the unique ecology and delicate balance of the living desert.

LEFT Namibia's desert-dwelling elephants have adapted to their harsh Kaokoland environment. This elephant browses on the indigenous Ana trees that dot the veld.

TOP Like all elephant cows, the mothers of desert herds are extremely protective of their young calves and will challenge any behaviour that may threaten their offspring.

ABOVE A lone bull crosses the dry riverbed of the Hoanib.

OPPOSITE AND OVERLEAF The relatively small but thriving population of what is commonly called the desert elephants may spend as long as four days without water, and travel in excess of 60 kilometres across the arid expanse in search of water.

LEFT The southern giraffe feeds on the leaves of trees that provide sustenance in the absence of water in the Hoanib River that only occasionally flows down this shallow stretch of land in the Kaokoveld. Many of the wild animals here will make their way from one water supply to another as the scarce water supplies dry up during the dry season.

TOP Most often found in the northern parts of Namibia – and virtually across Botswana – the red-billed francolin is a common resident of Kaokoland where, unlike many other francolins, it will happily feed on the open plains.

ABOVE Acclaimed as the continent's biggest lizard, the Nile or water monitor, at home in the waters of the Kunene River, can grow to as long as two metres.

OPPOSITE Herds of springbok cross the barren gravel plains of Kaokoland.

LEFT The Himba people of the northwest regions are people of Herero descent, who have chosen to make Kaokoland their home. Still remarkably isolated from Western influence, these subsistence farmers remain true to their customs, and many still don traditional dress in everyday life. Their only concession appears to be the box-like shape of their homes, which differ from the traditional hut shapes of the Herero.

ABOVE Himba women are most easily recognised by the ochre paste they wear not only as a cosmetic on their faces, but also in their hair as a protection from the harsh effects of the African sun. Even young girls are taught the intricate patterning and methods of hairstyling from an early age.

OPPOSITE In a region where cattle are both important as a source of food and an indication of social status, the horse is more than a simple convenience. Here, a young Himba man shows off his mount as a sign of his wealth.

LEFT A young Himba child is strapped to the back of his mother so that he can be taken with her as she goes about her daily business. Not only does this young mother wear the ochre hair-covering typical of her people, but her leather headdress also indicates her status as a married woman.

ABOVE LEFT If unattached and eligible for marriage, the young Himba man will wear no form of head cover, but once he is married, he will don the traditional headscarf to indicate his married status.

ABOVE RIGHT Like many groups who remain true to centuries of tradition and ritual, the Himba people continue to celebrate the festivals and customs of their ancestors, most of which have their origins in Herero tradition and often centre around music, song and dance.

OPPOSITE The campfire not only provides the means by which meals are prepared but often forms the centre of certain rituals and age-old traditions. Here, two young Himba couples prepare food together, but it would be the task of the mother of the family to tend the sacred fires.

LEFT This virtually leafless bottle tree, in the Kaokoveld, north of the Hoanib River, is endemic to northern Namibia.

TOP The welwitschia, with its flattened crown that produces only two true leaves during the course of its life, is an ancient plant that occurs in gravelly soils of the Namib.

ABOVE The delicate blooms of the South West edelweiss belie the hardy characteristics demanded by its unforgiving environment.

OPPOSITE The Hoanib only occasionally flows, but on its banks lies the Khowarib Schlucht, an oasis from which rises a spring that sometimes tumbles onto the river path.

LEFT Rüppell's korhaan is a near-endemic inhabitant of the dry gravel plains of Namibia's northwestern coastal stretch, where individuals or, more commonly, small groups may be spotted among the bushmangrasses of the Kaokoveld.

ABOVE The arid expanse of Damaraland is, in parts, covered with *Euphorbia damarana* and bushmangrass. The euphorbia, endemic to the region, produces a toxic latex.

OPPOSITE Although no longer found in such great numbers, springbok remain the most abundant of southern Africa's antelope species, and herds still graze on the spring grasses that sprout on the plains that flank the Hoanib River.

OVERLEAF LEFT The central Oshana region, one of the four regions that cover what was once known as Owambo, takes its name from the shallow water courses known locally as *oshana*. These pans are flooded in the wet season and are typical of the Owambo landscape.

OVERLEAF RIGHT The Owambo area, flat and apparently featureless, is nevertheless a fascinating wilderness of river – albeit so often too dry to warrant the name – and shrubland. Much of the countryside here, north of Etosha, has now been given over to agricultural lands planted with millet, sorghum and beans.

ABOVE The baobab – or upside-down tree – is a fairly common sight in the wider Owambo region.

ABOVE AND OPPOSITE Small stands of ivory palms grow in clumps in the Owambo region, and are found exclusively in these northern stretches of Namibia, both in the untamed wilderness and semi-rural areas.

Left Black-faced impala, related to the more common impala found elsewhere on the subcontinent, are easily identified by the characteristic flashes on their faces and the brownish colour of their coats. It is particularly in the rainy season, when the flowers bloom and the otherwise dry vegetation takes on the hue of green, that these and other mammals of the region are at their healthiest and most abundant.

Above The famous old fortification at Namutoni, originally erected in 1902, has seen no less than three reincarnations over the last century. Having fallen prey to various powers over the years, it was finally declared a national monument in the late 1950s and is today open to overnight guests.

Opposite Etosha National Park, in the northwest of the country, is a protected sanctuary not only for the rare black-faced impala – pictured here at the Klein Namutoni water hole – but also for the tiny Damara dik-dik and the colossal black rhino.

LEFT A springbok ram, with its typically twisted horns and characteristic blaze of black splashed along its flank, drinks from the Kalkheuwel water hole in the Etosha National Park.

ABOVE Namibia's wild animals depend entirely on the generosity of Mother Nature. In times of rain, drinking water is not too difficult to find, but when there has been very little rain, the last remaining water holes offer the only respite from the harsh African sun, and herds of springbok and other mammals head for the water.

OPPOSITE The viciously pointed set of horns atop the equine head of the gemsbok – known internationally as the oryx – is the antelope's most distinctive feature and is found on both the male and the female of the species. The male of this adult pair at the Chudob water hole is attempting to mate with the apparently unreceptive female.

TOP LEFT During the mating season, zebra stallions, intent on establishing the survival of their own brood in this inhospitable landscape, will fight over supremacy over the herd of females.

LEFT Tall and elegant, the cow of the greater kudu is usually found in small groups of about three individuals. They do not carry the characteristic twisted horns so notable in the males of the species.

ABOVE The endangered black rhinoceros remains one of the continent's rarest mammals, but is well represented in the Etosha National Park, and may often be seen at water holes such as that at Okaukuejo at night.

OPPOSITE Burchell's zebra are abundant at Etosha and, except for the fact that they have fewer and broader stripes, may well be confused with Hartmann's mountain zebra, which tend to be confined to the hilly western area around Otjovasandu.

LEFT In a land where water is so scarce, and vegetation is sparse, nutritious food is, of course, equally hard to come by. To accommodate its body's demands for minerals, this male giraffe supplements its dietary needs by sucking the bone from a carcass in order to extract the necessary minerals.

ABOVE AND OPPOSITE Giraffe bulls, with legs astride and necks flailing, fight for the attention of the female during the mating season. This usually takes place during the rains, when the vegetation of the surrounding countryside can accommodate the foraging of the breeding pairs and their offspring.

TOP LEFT Southern Africa is home to a huge population of weavers and a large percentage occur in Namibia – particularly the northern regions.

LEFT The lesser kestrel favours open grasslands and even the cultivated lands that cover so much of the Caprivi region.

ABOVE The vibrantly coloured lilac-breasted roller is a common resident of the savanna that stretches across much of the subcontinent, and may be spotted with some ease against the often sombre backdrop of Etosha.

OPPOSITE Swooping from a high rock crevice to the spiked branches of a thorn tree, the red-necked falcon – although not a common resident – may be found throughout Namibia, Botswana, Mozambique and the northern parts of South Africa.

TOP LEFT AND ABOVE Following the summer rains, the all-important water holes fill with the life-giving water so vital to wildlife. Not only is the water required for drinking, but the mud in which the elephants wallow help protect their thick skins from the searing heat.

CENTRE LEFT AND LEFT The survival of the fittest is perhaps the instinct that is most prominent here in the harsh wilderness of Namibia. Powerful bulls constantly challenge each other for domination over the cows.

OPPOSITE Elephants converge on the pans – be they water-filled or simple puddles – to drink every day in order to sustain their great, lumbering bodies in the oppressive heat. An individual may drink no less than 200 litres a day.

OVERLEAF LEFT Absent only in the far northern, western and southern regions of Namibia, cheetah may be found throughout the semi-desert and grasslands of central Namibia and, although numbers are low, the country boasts the largest population.

OVERLEAF RIGHT Widely distributed throughout sub-Saharan Africa, the status of the leopard is not threatened on the subcontinent, and Namibia has a secure population of its own.

The largest member of Africa's great cat family, the lion remains king of the beasts. These majestic creatures may hunt in pairs or family groups, but it is more often than not the lioness that provides the meal. She will wait amid the grasses that skirt a water hole, carefully approach her chosen victim and give chase and, with a terrifying combination of extraordinary power and strength, bring down her prey. The male, on the other hand, will be offered first pickings from the carcass, and the cubs will remain in the shadows until he has eaten his fill.

LEFT Subsistence farming is a way of life for most of the people of the northern Caprivi district, and their farming methods remain true to age-old traditions. This Mafwe woman of the western areas carries a basket filled with the distinctive *mahangu*, or millet, which is a vital contributor to the all-important crop production in the north.

ABOVE Many of the people of the rural areas, such as Lisikili in east Caprivi, have chosen to keep to ancient customs and rituals, and the region is studded with traditional villages that still follow the rigid structures of the past.

OPPOSITE Transport on the water courses is much like it is elsewhere in Africa, and *mokoros* (dugout canoes) ferry villagers up and down the Kwando River.

TOP LEFT Although the northern areas of the country are reserved almost entirely for the planting of food crops for the vast majority of Namibia's population, there are places along this upper stretch that do accommodate less practical pursuits. At Katima Mulilo, in the eastern Caprivi, speedboats flash by on the sometimes volatile waters of the great Zambezi River.

CENTRE LEFT Because water is generally scarce across Namibia, the few rivers that run throughout the year are not only a vital life-giving force, but also form centres around which Namibians play. Lianshulu on the Kwando River, in east Caprivi, offers safari boat trips down the river, from which guests view the game that wanders down to the water's edge.

LEFT If the adventure of a safari or a game drive cannot lure a traveller, a gentle cruise on the waters of the Zambezi may prove sufficient enticement. In recent years, the peace that followed the struggle for self-determination has also brought with it a steady growth in tourism to Namibia.

ABOVE The Kwando River, although hardly equal in stature to the mighty Zambezi and its often torrential waters, is a vital water source to the people of the Caprivi.

OPPOSITE The northeastern parts of the country is a wilderness of swamp, woodland and rivers – so unlike the typical image of Namibia. It is here that the Okavango River borders West Caprivi and reaches far into Botswana.

LEFT The area around Twyfelfontein, framed by the craggy overhangs of unique geological formations carved from sandstone, boasts one of the richest finds of ancient rock art on the continent.

ABOVE The savanna that surrounds the small town of Khoirixas in the Kunene district in the west of the country forms the setting for the rugged Ugab Valley, a vast and wild country studded with mopane and thornbush dominated by the 35-metre tower of Finger Rock.

OPPOSITE The rocky terraces of the Ugab Valley were chiselled from the land by violent forces of nature that swept across this landscape over thousands of years, giving rise to the exceptional shapes and crevices of this somewhat desolate region.

LEFT In an area where plant life is sparse and, where it does occur, is rather unimpressive, lies the wonder of what is known as the Petrified Forest, a series of fossilised trees dragged here millions of years ago, covered by sediment and then eroded to expose the unusual formations we see today.

ABOVE The rounded shape and massive boulders of the unique granite domes that flank the great Spitzkoppe near Usakos have given the Pondok mountains their name (*pondok* is the Afrikaans-Dutch word for 'hut').

OPPOSITE Damaraland is a region not blessed with an abundance of wildlife and many of those animals that do occur here depend on the delicate balance of the environment for survival. As a result, conservationists attached to the Save the Rhino effort keep vigilant watch and patrol the area to protect it from the threat of poachers.

TOP LEFT The Erongo mountain is what remains of an ancient volcano that once dominated the area, but it is the plains of the Ameib farm that surround this mountain that give rise to Elephant's Head, a granite formation protruding from the flatlands.

LEFT The short-toed rock thrush is a common resident across virtually the entire country, and may easily be spotted darting among the rocky slopes and vegetation of the Erongo.

ABOVE The exceptional collection of ancient rock engravings at Twyfelfontein, west of Khoirixas, is one of Africa's finest, and some of the petroglyphs – among them springbok, gemsbok, giraffe, zebra and rhino – depicted here date back nearly 5 000 years.

OPPOSITE Standing some 700 metres high above the arid savanna plains of Damaraland, the isolated granite massif of the Spitzkoppe forms an impressive backdrop to the town of Usakos.

OVERLEAF LEFT The Cape fur seals so abundant on the western coast of the subcontinent gather on the shore in about October every year. It is then that the cows in the bull's harem give birth to their pups and, barely a week later, mate again for the next season.

OVERLEAF RIGHT The lagoon around which lies the coastal town of Walvis Bay is home to such an impressive collection of water birds – sometimes numbering more than 60 000 birds – that it, along with adjoining wetlands and coastal stretch, has been proclaimed a nature reserve.

LEFT Although a modern town in every sense and the country's top holiday destination, Swakopmund – neatly sandwiched between the desert and the sea – has its origins in the heyday of German colonialism.

ABOVE Common throughout much of southern Africa, the grey heron, with its distinctive white neck and black crown feathers, is most often spotted around lagoons, estuaries and pans. Here they patrol the crest of a dune in the Namib-Naukluft.

OPPOSITE With the oppressive heat that pervades the land in the summer months, Namibians retreat to the milder climes of the coast and Swakopmund, which, in close proximity to both the sea and the dunes of the Namib, has become the country's recreational capital and a centre for recreational sports such as dune-surfing.

RIGHT Like so much of the colonial architecture that dominates the town, the Altes Amtsgericht, Swakopmund's old magistrate's building, was erected in the early 20th century, during a time when German colonial powers still presided over the town.

LEFT In a country that has seen the passing of many a foreign power through the pages of history, most Herero people remain true to ancient customs and have adapted relatively modern dress to conform to the traditions of old.

OPPOSITE Another remnant of the German heritage, still very prominent in Swakopmund today, is the Hohenzollernhaus, an elaborately decorated architectural gem constructed in 1906.

LEFT The capital at Windhoek is every inch a modern city, which has built on its colonial past to become the economic powerhouse of Namibia. Today, although this is seldom reflected in the pockets of ordinary citizens, the country boasts one of the highest per capita income rates in all of Africa.

ABOVE The national economy, centring around the capital city, depends almost exclusively on the export of its most vital resources, such as diamonds and base metals, and the products of the land, including beef and karakul pelts.

OPPOSITE A quiet oasis of palm trees in the centre of the city.

LEFT The informal economic sector is growing steadily in Windhoek, and particularly so with the burgeoning of the tourism market. Indigenous souvenirs, such as these being sold at the city's famed open-air curio market near the landmark Christuskirche, provide a valuable source of income for locals.

ABOVE AND OPPOSITE Having gained a new lease of life with independence in the late 20th century, Namibia is beginning to concentrate on the gradual rebuilding of its economy. One of the most important areas of development is the tourism industry, with hotels catering more and more for international travellers.

OVERLEAF LEFT The result of this rapid urbanisation has meant that cities such as Windhoek – backed by the magnificent Auas mountains – have grown remarkably over recent years.

OVERLEAF RIGHT Much of the highlying lands to the west of Rehoboth has been devoted to the farming of small stock such as sheep and goats, but the open expanses still erupt in a blaze of aloes and other indigenous vegetation after the rains.

LEFT AND ABOVE The wind-blown sand of the Namib creates mammoth dunes that stretch across the arid landscape, reaching crests that may extend as high as hundreds of metres. OPPOSITE A wild grape tree, resembling in appearance the distinctive baobab but entirely unrelated, is backed by the magnificence of the Spitzkoppe.

LEFT AND ABOVE Balloon trips are a popular alternative to the standard safari. The balloons glide effortlessly across the still air that hangs over the edge of the Namib, offering a rather different view of the great desert.

OPPOSITE An exclusive retreat in the desert, the plush Karos Sossusvlei Lodge is set amid the open sands of Sesriem on the edge of the Namib.

OVERLEAF LEFT The granite massif of the Witberge – the Afrikaans translation for 'white mountains' – in the heart of the Namib, reaches some 426 metres into the desert sky.

OVERLEAF RIGHT Although the Namib-Naukluft comprises an extraordinary array of varying landscapes, it is the corrugated dunes that are most characteristic of this desert region that lies between the Kuiseb River and the town of Lüderitz.

Wild horses, which in all probability are the descendants of those steeds originally abandoned by German troops in the early 1900s, have established a herd in the Namib. Although this feral herd has adapted rather well to the demanding conditions of the desert, individuals have on occasion struggled to survive exceptionally dry spells that pervade the land.

LEFT AND OPPOSITE Desert life is never easy, but the gemsbok is quite at home here. These hardy antelope, with their unique physiological adaptations for these harsh conditions, are usually found in herds of up to 30 individuals.

ABOVE The plants of the tsamma melons lie scattered across the sandy plains and dunes of the Namib, and the succulent fruits provide a vital source of moisture for many desert-dwelling animals.

OVERLEAF LEFT The dry riverbed of the Auob, punctuated occasionally by camel thorn trees, stretches along the ridged dunes that skirt the town of Aus.

OVERLEAF RIGHT The flooded Sossusvlei, one of the desert's most delicate ecosystems, comprises a shallow pan of water guarded by a barricade of dunes, which reach up no less than 325 metres in places.

LEFT In certain areas of the Namib-Naukluft, straggly grasses push through the sand on the edge of the desert to cover the dunes in scratchy patches of green.

TOP AND OPPOSITE The harsh sun extracts every drop of moisture from the arid land, leaving the few pans – such as this desolate shallow – without a drop, and even the hardiest desert trees struggle to survive.

ABOVE The undulating but relatively barren land that surrounds the town of Swakopmund is a lunar landscape of dry hillock and sandy dune.

LEFT Although the pans that have formed in the canyon carved by the Tsauchab River fill with water during the brief rainy season, both the pools and the river are little more than dustbowls in the dry months.

ABOVE The gravel and quartz plains of the expansive Namib-Naukluft Park extend right up to the coastal dunes dotted periodically by stands of camel thorn trees.

OPPOSITE On the edge of the great Namib stand the magnificent Naukluft mountains, which together comprise the impressive escarpment that neatly separates the wave-lashed shore from the dry interior that forms the desert.

LEFT From the air, the dry bed of the Tsauchab River appears little more than a lifeless ribbon snaking through an equally parched landscape.
OPPOSITE On a coast battered by the relentless waves of the Atlantic, life is precarious to say the least and many a vessel has met its fate on this treacherous shore. In 1976, the doomed *Shaunee* floundered in the violent waves off the coast from Walvis Bay.

RIGHT The vast lagoon of Sandwich Harbour, less than 50 kilometres from Walvis Bay, is one of the continent's most valuable wetland areas and, despite the rather sudden disappearance of its freshwater pools in recent years, remains home to a constant parade of avifauna.

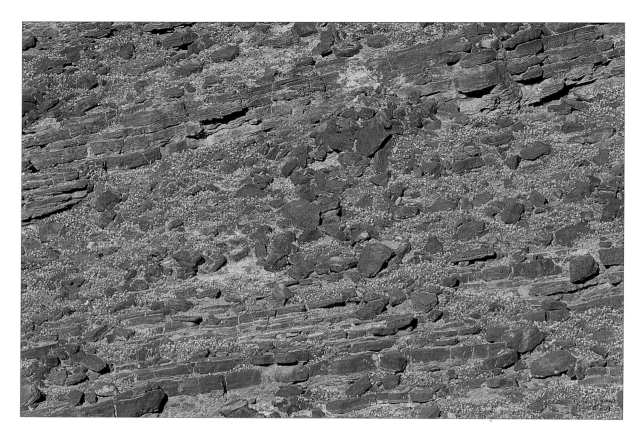

TOP LEFT Like all of the hardy vegetation at home in the harsh desert environment, the spindly plains aloe has adapted to accommodate the extremely arid conditions of this unforgiving landscape.

CENTRE LEFT Perhaps to spite the sea of sand that surrounds it and the apparent lifelessness of its environment, the pretty flowers of the *Tribulus* species bring life and colour to the Namib.

LEFT The rather unusual shapes and configurations of the many succulent species at home in the desert landscape, such as this *Augea capensis* near Lüderitz, add a new dimension to the flora of the Namib.

ABOVE The all-too-infrequent rains offer welcome respite to the dormant vegetation of the desert, and when the rain does come, it brings with it a brief explosion of colour on the otherwise empty rockland.

OPPOSITE In the fleeting period of rains, the red dunes of the southern Namib are covered with carpets of yellow *Tribulus* flowers and delicate green grasses, which will survive for only a short while.

LEFT AND ABOVE As if to reclaim its sovereignty over a land for so long colonised by diamond prospectors, the winds and sands of the Namib have again taken over the town of Kolmanskop, once the vital centre of the country's lucrative diamond-mining industry.

OPPOSITE Kolmanskop, east of Lüderitz, lies abandoned after the last of its diamonds were mined in 1956. Slowly, the desert is reclaiming its territories and the grand homes of the once-prosperous community, first established by German prospectors in 1908, are engulfed by waves of creeping sand.

OVERLEAF LEFT Shrouded in coastal fog or lashed by the menacing ocean, the 30-metre structure of the landmark Bogenfels rock arch in the restricted Diamond Area 1 south of Lüderitz reaches down into the Atlantic that has carved its unique shape.

OVERLEAF RIGHT As the main focus of the country's diamond industry, Lüderitz is a typical industrial town. Although there is little to offer the adventurer, it is nevertheless steeped in a fascinating past. Prominent among its historical landmarks is the famed Evangelical Lutheran Church (Felsenkirche), erected in 1912.

LEFT A single *Aloe littoralis* protrudes from the rocky veld, sprinkled with the yellow flowers of the *Tribulus* species found within the Quiver Tree Forest near Keetmanshoop.

TOP Despite the dangers of the toxic latex produced by the *Euphorbia virosa* below it, a flock of sociable weavers has built their huge communal nest in the ragged branches of a quiver tree.

ABOVE The quiver tree, or *kokerboom*, can grow as high as nine metres and, between May and July, it will give rise to dense clusters of bright yellow blooms.

OPPOSITE Although quiver trees don't usually grow in groves, some 200 may be found together in the Quiver Tree Forest near Keetmanshoop, which carries an image of the tree on its emblem.

ABOVE One of the most prolific game species in the Hardap Game Reserve that adjoins the recreation resort of the same name is Hartmann's mountain zebra, a subspecies of the Cape mountain zebra found only in this arid part of the subcontinent.

OPPOSITE The smelly shepherd's tree – a characteristic shrub-like tree typical of the rocky outcrops of Namibia's semi-desert areas such as Hardap – takes its common name from the sharp and pungent smell of its flowers and freshly cut branches.

Having occupied this land for centuries, the San of what is commonly referred to as Bushmanland even today, have learned to make good use of its resources. Although, through the years and amid increasing Westernisation, most of the members of this indigenous group have left behind the customs of the past, small clusters still live much as they have for hundreds of years. One such group is the Kung Bushmen of the Intu Afrika Kalahari Game Reserve, who are benefiting from a development project intent on preserving the tradition of the local San.

OPPOSITE Although the sandy tracks first cut through the Kalahari wilderness by the likes of David Livingstone in the 1800s have given way to a considerably more impressive infrastructure in parts, gravel roads are still the paths more travelled in the Kalahari.

LEFT The nearly 400 000-hectare Kaudom Game Reserve boasts an extraordinary diversity of wildlife, principal among which is the great king of the beasts, the lion.

TOP Ever on the lookout, an alert suricate stands guard atop a thornbush in the vast expanse of the Kalahari.

ABOVE Two playful young Cape ground squirrels cavort on the sands of the Kalahari. When the sun becomes unbearable, they will hoist their tails and shelter under their own shade.

OPPOSITE The bat-eared fox is a fairly common sight throughout the Kalahari and indeed much of the western parts of southern Africa. This shy, largely nocturnal creature is typically found on the open plains and in sparsely wooded areas of the Kalahari.

LEFT Near-endemic to southern Africa, the pale chanting goshawk favours the arid areas of the subcontinent and it is not uncommon to see it flitting across the sky of the dry western regions, where its distinctly harmonious call may often be heard.

ABOVE The male ground agama develops shades of blue on the throat and the sides of the head during the breeding season in order to attract the attention of females.

OPPOSITE Although the searing heat of the desert is most often the cause for concern, the animals and birds of the Kalahari, such as the Marico flycatcher, often have to take precautions against the icy cold that permeates the air on winter mornings.

Left This young Gabar goshawk may be distinguished from other hawks by its grey throat patch and white rump. These birds are locally common in the northern reaches of southern Africa and prefer as their habitat the semi-arid regions typical of Namibia.

Above The thatch-like structure in the crown of this thorn tree is the communal nest of sociable weavers, gregarious birds that usually flock together for security.

Opposite Sociable weavers are fairly common residents of the dry thornveld and woodlands of the central and western regions of southern Africa.

LEFT From the tip of the strangely elongated structure of *Trichocaulon alstoni,* found in the arid surroundings of the Namib, blooms of yellow emerge to brighten up the rockface.

TOP AND OPPOSITE   The smooth, mushroom-shaped flower of the *Hoodia macrantha* on the banks of the Orange River stands in contrast to the rough and thorny stem.

ABOVE Flowers of *Tribulus* litter the vicinity of the Fish River Canyon after the seasonal rains.

Second only in stature to the Grand Canyon in the USA, the steep ravines and rugged inclines of Namibia's Fish River Canyon remain one of the most remarkable geological features of the continent. Eroded through time by the powerful forces of nature and the flow of the Fish River, these remarkable rock surfaces are studded with desert-dwelling plants such as the *Aloe gariepensis* (foreground, above) and other succulents typical of this exceptionally dry region of the Nama Karoo.

OVERLEAF Masses of *Euphorbia gregaria* cover the dusk landscape in the area of the Fish River Canyon.